A PERSONAL GROWTH JOURNAL

FOR DISCOVERING
YOUR POWERFUL

PASSION IN LIFE

THIS BOOK BELONGS TO

____

____

____

BOOK DETAILS:

Continued from book: ________________

Your journal start date: ________________

Your journal end date: ________________

Continued to book: ________________

BLOOM WITH *Grace*

We are so grateful for your kind words. Thanks for sharing your review with us and the community.

Table of Contents

Make your passion profession

Part 1 Discover Your True Self

Part 2 It' s time to switch off

Part 3 Find Greater Success With Self-Knowledge

Part 4 Discover your passion

Table of Contents

Notes

Make your
PASSION
your
PROFESSION

DISCOVERING YOUR TRUE PASSION

Many of us go through life with interests that we never truly nurture and enjoy because we are too concerned about what others think. Of course, that's no way to live!

Finding your passion is an important part of self-discovery. You will be a happier, more balanced individual when you find and develop your passions. Your whole life will change before your eyes!

Finding Your Passion

You may think that finding your passion is easier said than done, and it is for many people. However, you can find your passion in two easy steps:

1. Set your mind to finding your passion

Once you focus on your pursuit of passion, your mind will be attuned to anything that will contribute to the solution.

2. Use an effective mind tool

There is a well-known tool you can use to help you along the way if you are afraid to branch out and follow your dreams. You can also use this tool to keep going down the right path to find what you are interested in. What is this handy tool? It's embracing your passion through affirmations!

AFFIRMATIONS CAN HELP YOU PUSH THROUGH YOUR SELF-DOUBTS AND HELP LEAD YOU TO A MORE PASSIONATE LIFE.

What Are Passion Affirmations?

Many people hear the term passion affirmations and wonder what affirmations could possibly be, and why they should use them. Passion affirmations are statements that will activate your brain to focus on and attain the goals you set for yourself

These statements often are descriptive of the feelings or behaviors you would like to possess in any given situation. They may remind you about your self-worth or the importance of your passions

How Can You Use Passion Affirmations?

Passion affirmations can be used in moments when you might be having some negative inner dialogue, or when you are second-guessing your desire to pursue your passions. In those moments of doubt, you may want to use a passion affirmation like, I have no need to do what others think I should. I am strengthened by doing the things I love to do. You'll want to believe this even if it's a challenge in the beginning.

You are reaffirming the statement and making it your personal truth every time you say your passion affirmation out loud.

There are also passion affirmations that can help you overcome guilt that you may feel when you indulge in your passion. We all have a right to pursue our passions, as long as they are in balance with our responsibilities. There is nothing wrong with pursuing a passion. You deserve to spend time on you

When you are having one of those days where you feel guilty for enjoying your favorite hobby or past time you can say, I am actively involved in my hobbies. It gives me energy and strength after a hard day.

You are giving your mind permission to replace negative thoughts with positive ones when you use affirmations

Passion affirmations not only help you discover your passions but also enable you to live a more passionate life. This positive dialogue will become second nature in time as it pushes out negative feelings and self-doubt. Being passionate is a way of expressing love for yourself. You should indulge in your passions and remember that they are good for you and those around you.

Note:

PURPOSE IN LIFE DIAGRAM

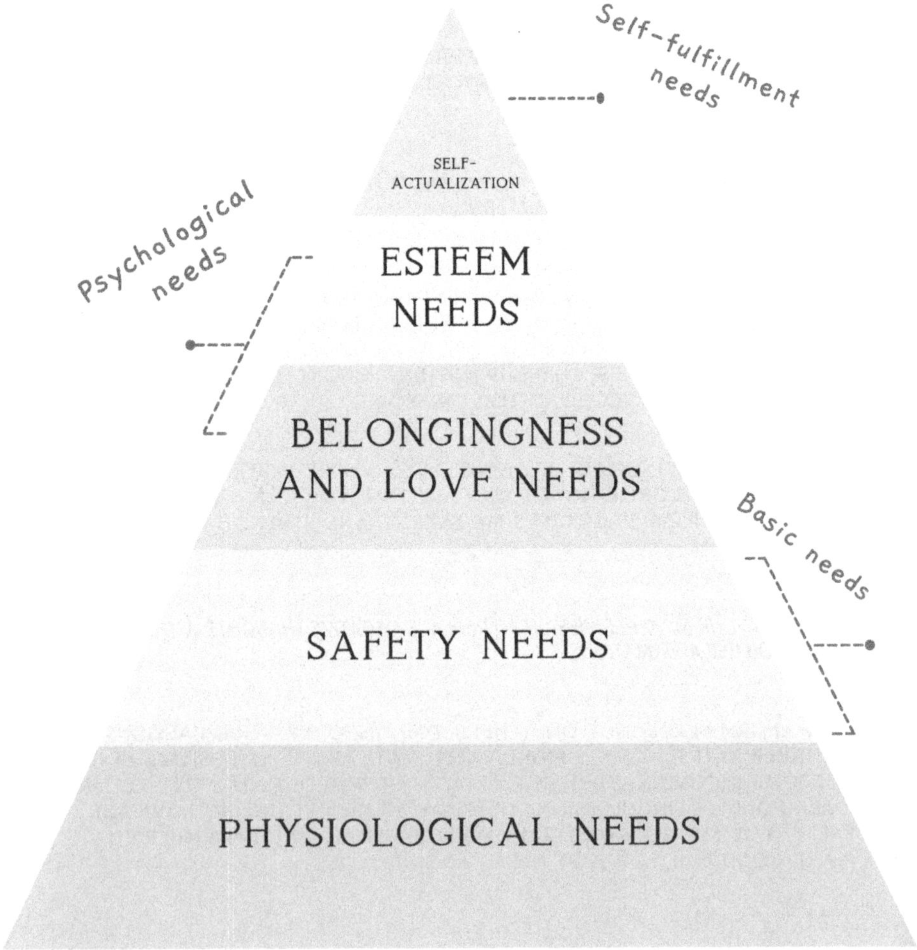

HOW TO DISCOVER YOUR PASSION

- Is there something you already love to do?
- What do you read hundreds of pages about?
- Research as much as possible
- Try it first
- Practice, practice, and practice
- Never give up

Part 1

Discover Your True Self

GETTING TO KNOW MYSELF

ANSWER THE FOLLOWING QUESTIONS. THERE ARE NO RULES. JUST LET YOUR HEART SPEAK.

AM I TRULY HAPPY AND AT PEACE WITH MYSELF? WHY? WHY NOT?

WHAT IS MY "HIGHER SELF" LIKE? DESCRIBE IN DETAIL.

THOUGHT PATTERN

START MONITORING YOUR THOUGHT PATTERNS. WRITE DOWN NEGATIVE THOUGHTS AND REPLACE EACH AND EVERY NEGATIVE THOUGHT WITH POSITIVE ONES.

NEGATIVE

POSITIVE

NEGATIVE

POSITIVE

NEGATIVE

POSITIVE

NEGATIVE

POSITIVE

9

LIMITING BELIEFS

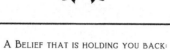

A Belief that is holding you back:

" ex. I can't change myself."

Where did this belief come from?

How is this belief harmful?

What is a better alternative for this belief?

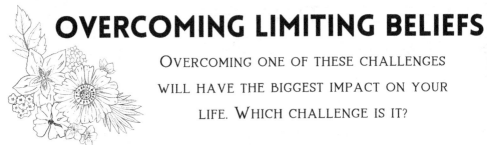

OVERCOMING LIMITING BELIEFS

Overcoming one of these challenges will have the biggest impact on your life. Which challenge is it?

OVERCOMING LIMITING BELIEFS

WHAT POSITIVE BELIEFS WOULD BE BETTER FOR HELPING YOU ATTAIN YOUR GOALS? FOR EACH NEGATIVE BELIEF THAT'S HOLDING YOU BACK, COME UP WITH A POSITIVE BELIEF THAT WOULD SUPPORT YOUR DESIRES.

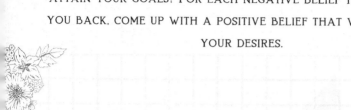

How To Turn Failure Into Success

What challenges in my life right now are caused by my fear of failure? What would I do if I weren't afraid of failure?

13

Self Acceptance

How content am I with my life right now? How well do I accept myself and my current situation? Can I see how my lack of self-acceptance and my lack of contentment are related?

What's Your Mood Right Now?

Women often paint how they feel. They use bright colors when they feel happy or excited. Some use thick, heavy lines when they're sad or angry.

Create your mood portrait below. Use different lines, colors, and shapes and decorate the head to express how you feel.

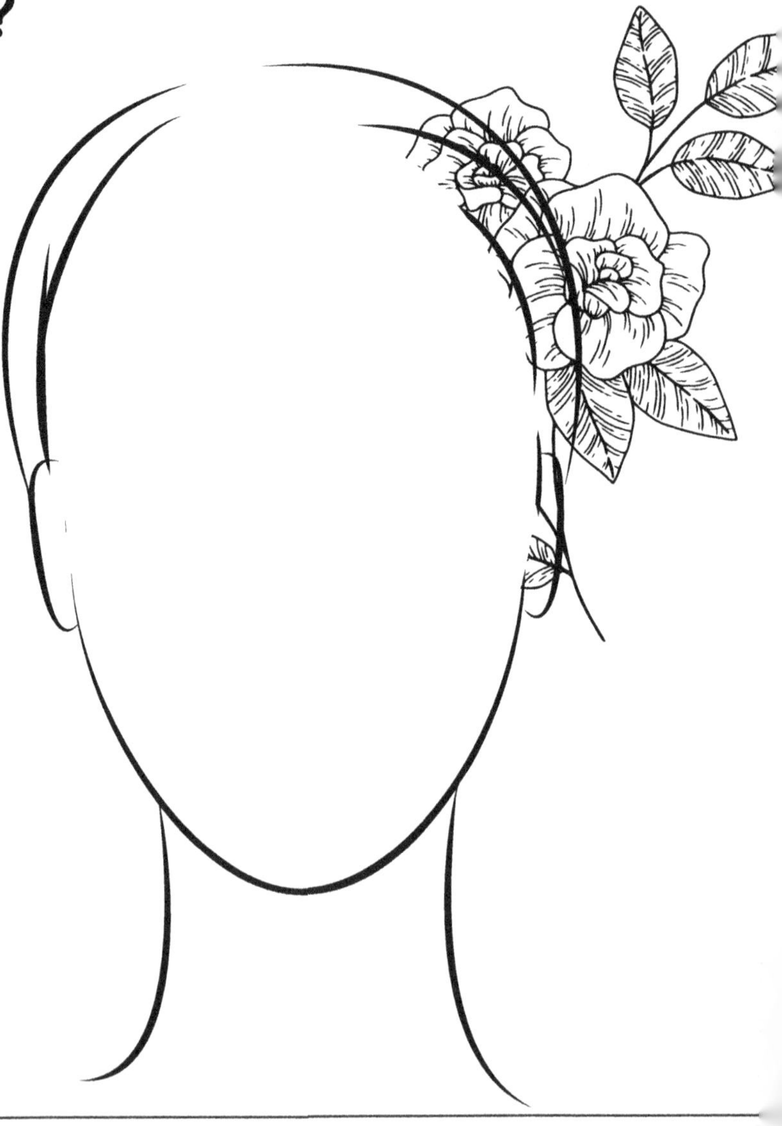

NOTES :

RAISE YOUR VIBRATION

One person with whom you share your adventures:

One meal that reminds you of home:

One memory that makes you gigle:

One errand you're always up for:

One thing you believe now more than ever:

One kind of surprise that brightens your day:

One music that you love to listen:

INSPIRATIONS

PODCASTS	BOOKS

SONGS	VIDEOS

COURSES	AUDIO

VISION BOARD

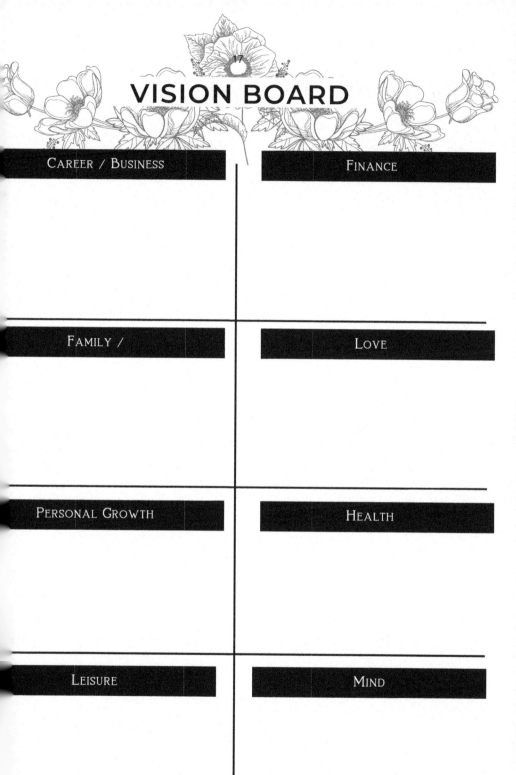

Career / Business	Finance

Family /	Love

Personal Growth	Health

Leisure	Mind

My Notes

Part 2

It's time to switch off

Hi Guys!

Let me ask you a question: when was the last time you switched everything off and simply sat, purposely switching off from the world? Don't worry if it's been a while!

These days, we live in a world of screens, social media, and information that is instantly available, from pretty much anywhere. This means that, even if we feel like we're relaxing, our brains are constantly on the go. We are always stimulated by some kind of information.

It's time to switch off!

The point of this journal is to get you to switch off for 10-30 minutes everyday for 45 days! You can then record your "switch off" time for reflection and to see how beneficial it has been for you over time

On the next pages you'll find instructions on how to use this journal. After that, it is over to you.

Enjoy switching off!

How To Use This Part

- CHOOSE A TIME OF DAY WHEN YOU'RE LEAST LIKELY TO BE DISTURBED
- CHOOSE A QUIET PLACE WHERE YOU'LL BE COMFORTABLE AND RELAXED.
- CHOOSE A FEW THINGS THAT MIGHT MAKE YOUR SWITCH OF TIME NICER.
- SET A TIMER FOR BETWEEN 10-30 MINUTES (DON'T WATCH THE CLOCK)
- YOU MIGHT FIND IT HARD TO SWITCH OFF TO BEGIN WITH. SO, YOU MIGHT LIKE TO START WITH 10 MINUTES A DAY AND BUILD UP OVER TIME.
- TAKE SOME DEEP BREATHES AND RELAX.
- JUST SIT AND TAKE NOTE OF HOW YOU FEEL, WHAT YOU SEE, AND WHAT YOU NOTICE. YOU'LL PROBABLY FIND YOU NOTICED MORE ABOUT YOURSELF AND YOUR SURROUNDINGS DURING THIS TIME.
- TRY NOT TO LOOK AT ANY SCREENS, READ, WATCH OR LISTEN TO ANYTHING DURING THIS TIME UNLESS 100% NECESSARY.
- IF YOU NEED TO, LISTEN TO CALMING MUSIC. MAYBE COLORING OR DOODLING MIGHT HELP, TOO.
- FILL IN THE JOURNAL PAGES EACH DAY TO HELP YOU REFLECT
- FILL IN THE QUICK LOG PAGES TO HELP KEEP TRACK OF YOUR PROGRESS.
- USE THE PAGES AT THE BACK IF YOU NEED MORE ROOM FOR REFLECTION
- TRY AND SWITCH OFF EVERY DAY FOR 45 DAYS.

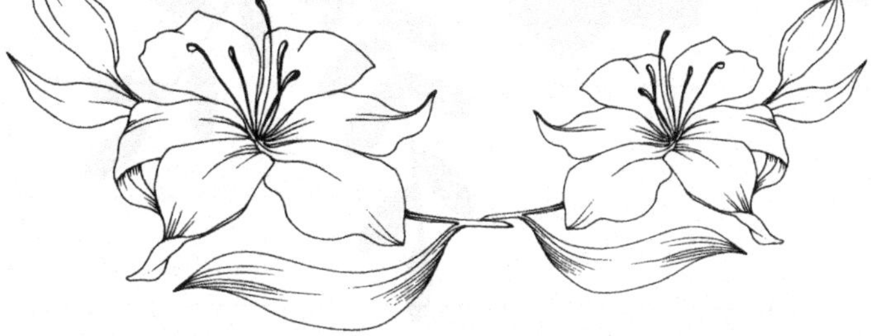

Things To Make My Switch Off Nicer

Candles	☐
Cushions	☐
Blankets	☐
Incense	☐
Essential oils	☐
Calming music/sounds	☐
Guided meditations	☐
Nice views	☐
Coloring books/doodle pads	☐
	☐
	☐
	☐
	☐
	☐
	☐
	☐
	☐
	☐
	☐

DIGITAL DETOX

DIGITAL DETOX JOURNAL

1. What will you do to prepare yourself for your detox, so you'll know what to expect?

2. Write your personalized detox plan. Set the rules and duration for your digital detox. Be reasonable for greater success.

DIGITAL DETOX JOURNAL

3. Make a list of every type of notification you get. Then, turn them all off.

4. How will you restrict your access to social media websites?

5. Make a list of everyone you want to notify about your detox, so they'll know why you're not posting on social media or responding to emails or texts.

6. What social engagements would you like to plan so that you can reconnect with friends or family while you're detoxing?

DIGITAL DETOX JOURNAL

7. MAKE ALTERNATE PLANS FOR THINGS THAT YOU USUALLY CHECK YOUR PHONE FOR, SUCH AS THE TIME. WHERE WILL YOU GET A WRISTWATCH - AN EASY FIX TO HELP YOU KEEP AWAY FROM YOUR PHONE?

8. WHAT BOOKS WOULD YOU BE INTERESTED IN CHECKING OUT FROM THE LIBRARY TO READ WHILE YOU HAVE EXTRA TIME? IS THERE SOMETHING THAT YOU WOULD LIKE TO LEARN ABOUT?

9. Choose a detox partner. Make a list of the possibilities and go down the list one by one until you find your accountability and support partner.

10. Plan activities or hobbies that you can enjoy with your extra time during your detox.

DIGITAL DETOX JOURNAL

11. What obstacles do you think you're likely to encounter that could stall or derail your detox? How could you overcome these obstacles?

BENEFITS OF THIS DETOX

MAKE A LIST OF THE BENEFITS THAT YOU'VE RECEIVED FROM THIS DETOX:

Mental health benefits:

Physical health benefits:

Relationship benefits – reconnecting with friends and family:

Benefits from having more free time:

BENEFITS OF THIS DETOX

MAKE A LIST OF THE BENEFITS THAT YOU'VE RECEIVED FROM THIS DETOX:

Benefits from greater focus and longer attention span:

Productivity benefits:

Enhanced social skills from reconnecting with the "real" world:

Notes

DOODLE PAGE

Part 3

Find Greater Success With Self-Knowledge

FIND GREATER SUCCESS WITH SELF-KNOWLEDGE

Knowing oneself is one of the more challenging tasks a person can undertake. When you know yourself intimately,

success becomes more certain. It's easier to predict the areas in which you will struggle.

Knowing your strengths, weaknesses, and preferences allows you to set more achievable goals and manage yourself more skillfully.

Answer these questions to gain a better perspective of how to use and grow your intuition and apply it to your life.

What are my greatest strengths? How do I know? How can I use my strengths to be more successful?

Beauty & strength come from within

WHAT ARE MY GREATEST WEAKNESSES? HOW CAN I AVOID THESE WEAKNESSES OR STRENGTHEN THESE SKILLS?

Saying "no" is okay

What is my dream career? What makes it so appealing to me?

WHAT ARE MY MOST IMPORTANT VALUES? DOES MY BEHAVIOR REFLECT MY VALUES?

WHAT IS MY NUMBER ONE DESIRED ACHIEVEMENT IN LIFE? WHY?

WHAT THE BIGGEST MISTAKES I MAKE REPEATEDLY? HOW HAVE THESE MISTAKES COST ME?

Self Critical Thoughts And Boost Your Self Esteem

*Boosting your self-esteem first *

LOW SELF-ESTEEM IS UNFORTUNATELY A SELF-FULLING PROPHECY. THE WORSE YOU FEEL ABOUT WHO YOU ARE AND WHAT YOU DO, THE LESS MOTIVATION YOU'LL HAVE TO DO WHAT IT TAKES TO BUILD YOUR SELF-ESTEEM.

FROM THERE IT'S EASY TO SPIRAL DOWN INTO A CYCLE OF NEGATIVE AND CIRCULAR THINKING, KEEPING YOU MIRED IN DAMAGING AND ERRONEOUS BELIEFS.

HOW CAN YOU STOP THIS VICIOUS CYCLE AND START MOVING YOURSELF IN A MORE POSITIVE DIRECTION?

IT'S A PROCESS, AND IT WON'T HAPPEN OVERNIGHT, BUT THERE ARE THINGS YOU CAN DO TO GET IT STARTED AND KEEP IT MOVING. HERE ARE 6 QUESTIONS POWERFUL WAYS TO IMPROVE YOUR SELF-ESTEEM QUICKLY IN ORDER TO START FEELING MORE CONFIDENT.

Reframe Self-Critical Thoughts and Boost Your Self-Esteem

WHAT ARE THE MOST COMMON SELF-CRITICAL THOUGHTS YOU HAVE EVERY DAY?

Reframe Self-Critical Thoughts and Boost Your Self-Esteem

HOW CAN YOU LEARN TO REFRAME THESE NEGATIVE THOUGHTS?

Reframe Self-Critical Thoughts and Boost Your Self-Esteem

WHAT HAPPENS IN YOUR MIND AFTER A FAILURE OR DIFFICULT EXPERIENCE?

Reframe Self-Critical Thoughts and Boost Your Self-Esteem

WHAT CAN YOU DO TO HANDLE THESE DIFFICULT EXPERIENCES DIFFERENTLY, SO SELF-CRITICAL THOUGHT DECREASE?

Reframe Self-Critical Thoughts and Boost Your Self-Esteem

COMPARE YOUR SELF-CRITICAL THOUGHTS WITH THE POSITIVE ONES. HOW DO THEY EACH MAKE YOU FEEL?

Reframe Self-Critical Thoughts and Boost Your Self-Esteem

What can you do each day to fight self-critical thoughts?

My Notes

Part 4

Discover your passion

How To Use This Part

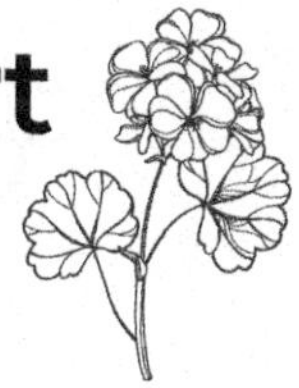

- Sit down in a quiet place. Get comfortable and focus on your breathing.
- After a couple of minutes, imagine yourself in 3-5 years doing what you love to do "fulfilling your purpose".
- Spend five minutes or more just observing.
- Next, answer the questions below after you finish this visualization exercise.

WAYS TO DISCOVER YOUR PASSION

Discovering your passion and being able to put it into words is important. Only then can you do the things that truly fulfill you.

Try these 25 techniques for discovering your passion:

1. Meditate
2. List everything that makes you happy
3. Tune other people out
4. Ask those who know you best
5. Take a class
6. What items interest you when you read?
7. What do you find easy?
8. Avoid letting monetary concerns limit your dreams
9. Talk to people who love the same things you do
10. Walk down memory lane. What did you love as a child?
11. Imagine your perfect day
12. If you only had one wish, what would it be?
13. Make a Passion Board
14. Visualize
15. What would you like to do in your free time?
16. Discover your creativity
17. Ask a friend to read your face as they list many items you might enjoy
18. Think about things you would do for free
19. Get involved in new activities or clubs that you feel might interest you
20. Listen to that small voice inside you to discover your true feelings
21. What gives you endless energy?
22. Do something you love every day
23. Research
24. Practice anything that interests you to discover more talents
25. Never give up

Notes

Passion and Purpose Visualization Exercise

What do you like to do? Are you sitting at a computer? Teaching a class? Playing video games? Participating in a strike? Meditating?

Passion and Purpose Visualization Exercise

WHAT IS GOING ON AROUND YOU? IS IT QUIET? LOUD? DARK? STILL? ARE THERE OTHER PEOPLE? IF SO, WHAT ARE THEY DOING? ARE PEOPLE ROWDY? SILENT? LAUGHING? STUDYING? TAKE IN THE ENVIRONMENT.

Passion and Purpose Visualization Exercise

What is going on around you? Is it quiet? Loud? Dark? Still? Are there other people? If so, what are they doing? Are people rowdy? Silent? Laughing? Studying? Take in the environment.

Passion and Purpose Visualization Exercise

Who/what is there? Are there children? Adults? Couples? Cats? Dogs? Mountains? Rain?

How are you interacting with them? Sitting with them in an audience? Talking one-on- one? Lecturing at a podium? Climbing a mountain? Watching a movie or concert?

Passion and Purpose Visualization Exercise

Are you at work? A home office? Sitting in your living room in your PJs? Walking a dog? Stroking a cat? Driving a car? Hugging your child? Kissing your spouse?

Pay attention to the details. What else do you notice? Feelings? Smells? Sounds? Sights? Tastes?

YOUR MISSION STATEMENT

In the space below write a mission statement that includes the following:

Example:

Who You Help: I help middle school kids

End Result: become well-adjusted adults

How: by teaching the core values of self-discipline, respect for others, focus, practice, patience, endurance, and self-care through karate

Why: to build leaders for future generations

Personal Mission Statement:

I help middle school kids become well-adjusted adults by teaching the core values of self-discipline, respect for others, focus, practice, patience, endurance, master and self-care through karate to build leaders for future generations.

Tip: Keep it brief and memorable. Your Personal Mission Statement should briefly describe your purpose and your personal call to action for this life in just 1 or 2 sentences.

Who You Help:	
End Result:	
How:	
Why:	

Notes :

MISSION STATEMENT

LIFE PURPOSE

Here are some questions to help you identify your purpose in life. Consider each of these and note your responses.

What are you most proud of having accomplished at this point in your life?

If you were financially able to retire one year from today, what would you begin working on to prepare for that?

LIFE PURPOSE

Here are some questions to help you identify your purpose in life. Consider each of these and note your responses.

If you could solve a world problem, what would it be?

What is the inkling you have of your purpose or vision?

LIFE PURPOSE

Here are some questions to help you identify your purpose in life. Consider each of these and note your responses.

If you could do anything you want, what would you most like to do in the next decade?

List three possible life purposes.

CREATING THE LIFE YOU LOVE

COMPLETE THIS WORKSHEET TO HELP YOU APPLY THESE SELF-COMPASSION CONCEPTS TO YOUR OWN LIFE. IMAGINE LIVING YOUR BEST LIFE AND LEARN HOW TO APPLY IT BY THINKING ABOUT AND THOUGHTFULLY ANSWERING THE QUESTIONS THAT FOLLOW. BY CONTINUING THIS PRACTICE, YOU WILL FIND GREATER FEELINGS OF SELF-LOVE AND EMPOWERMENT.

Clear Out All Areas of Doubt

WHAT IS ONE AREA OF DOUBT IN YOUR LIFE? WRITE 3- 4 SENTENCES ABOUT WHY YOU DOUBT WHAT YOU DO AND HOW YOU MIGHT MOVE FORWARD FROM IT.

HOW OFTEN DO YOU SACRIFICE YOUR NEEDS FOR WHAT OTHERS WANT?

CREATING THE LIFE YOU LOVE

Complete this worksheet to help you apply these self-compassion concepts to your own life. Imagine living your best life and learn how to apply it by thinking about and thoughtfully answering the questions that follow. By continuing this practice, you will find greater feelings of self-love and empowerment.

Clear Out All Areas of Doubt

Do you frequently apologize for things you do not need to apologize for?

Notes:

CREATING THE LIFE YOU LOVE

HAVE YOU EVER BEEN CALLED OR REFERRED TO YOURSELF AS A PEOPLE PLEASER? WHEN?

DO YOU STOP YOURSELF FROM SPEAKING UP FOR YOURSELF? WHEN?

AVOID OVERTHINKING

WHAT IS ONE REGRET YOU WOULD LIKE TO FULLY LET GO OF NOW?

WHAT WILL YOUR LIFE LOOK LIKE WHEN YOU'VE FINALLY RELEASED THIS REGRET?

WRITE DOWN TWO NEGATIVE THINGS YOU FREQUENTLY SAY TO YOURSELF. NEXT TO THOSE PHRASES, WRITE POSITIVE ONES THAT YOU CAN SAY INSTEAD.

EXPLORE COMMUNITY

WHAT IS ONE THING YOU ARE EXCITED TO TRY IN YOUR COMMUNITY? WHEN ARE YOU GOING TO PARTICIPATE IN THIS ACTIVITY?

WHAT INSPIRES YOU RIGHT NOW? WHAT MAKES YOU FEEL LIKE YOU CAN DO ANYTHING? WHAT IS YOUR BIGGEST SORCE OF INSPIRATION?

PRACTICE MINDFULNESS

How do you feel about sitting with the present moment, without jumping to action? Is this something that is difficult for you? Write 4-5 sentences describing your feelings about tolerating the moment, no matter how frustrating.

What is one mindfulness activity you would like to try? How are you going to make this activity part of your daily life?

Are there entire parts of your days that are unpleasant? Or entire parts of your months? During these unpleasant times, what will you do to remain self-compassionate? How will you remind yourself to keep practicing self-compassion?

LET GO OF WHAT HOLDS YOU BACK

LIST TWO RESENTMENTS THAT YOU ARE READY TO LET GO OF NOW. AS YOU WRITE THEM DOWN, IMAGINE THEM DISAPPEARING FROM YOUR HEART AND LEAVING LOVE IN ITS PLACE.

WHAT IS A BOUNDARY YOU ARE READY TO SET? FIRST, WRITE DOWN SOMETHING YOU NEED MORE OR LESS OF IN YOUR LIFE. NEXT, WRITE THE BOUNDARY THAT WILL HELP YOU STRUCTURE YOUR LIFE IN A WAY TO GET WHAT YOU NEED.

HOLD ON TO WHAT MOVES YOU FORWARD

List three of your values below.

Now, list one action per value that demonstrates each of those values.

HOLD ON TO WHAT MOVES YOU FORWARD

WHAT IS ONE WAY IN WHICH YOU CONNECT WITH YOUR SPIRITUALITY, NO MATTER HOW DEVELOPED?

WRITE FOUR SENTENCES BELOW THAT DESCRIBE TWO OF YOUR FAVORITE THINGS ABOUT YOURSELF.

VISION BOARD

DOODLE PAGE

Part 5

Action Is The Foundational Key To Success

DREAM BIG ACT NOW

MAKING BIG CHANGES IN YOUR LIFE CAN BE ACCOMPLISHED WITH QUICK AND EASY ACTIONS.

A DREAM *YOU* DREAM ALONE IS *ONLY A* DREAM

A DREAM YOU *DREAM* TOGETHER IS *REALITY*

PREPARING YOURSELF FOR ANY CHANGES IN YOUR LIFE CAN ENHANCE THE ODDS OF SUCCESS.

SMALL CHANGES-BIG IMPACT

The small change affects your life in so many ways! Use this worksheet to build your new impact. Think about it, how well do you understand yourself?

Which part of my life would have the biggest impact if I made the decision to change it?

What quick and easy actions could I take to bring about the changes I seek?

Which action can I focus on incorporating first? What progression, if any, should I use?

SMALL CHANGES-BIG IMPACT

THE SMALL CHANGE AFFECTS YOUR LIFE IN SO MANY WAYS! USE THIS WORKSHEET TO BUILD YOUR NEW IMPACT. THINK ABOUT IT, HOW WELL DO YOU UNDERSTAND YOURSELF?

HOW CAN I TURN THIS ACTION INTO A HABIT? BE SPECIFIC

WHAT IS THE NEXT STRONG HABIT I CAN BEGIN TO BUILD THAT WILL BE QUICK AND EASY FOR ME?

HOW CAN MAKING SMALLER CHANGES BE MORE EFFECTIVE THAN MY ATTEMPTS TO INSTITUTE MAJOR CHANGES IN THE PAST?

SELF-REGULATION

PRACTICE SELF-SOOTHING: WHAT ARE SOME POSITIVE WAYS THAT YOU CAN COUNT ON TO UPLIFT YOUR MOOD? WHAT ARE SOME MORE WAYS THAT YOU WOULD LIKE TO TRY?

PRACTICE SELF-DISCIPLINE: WHAT ARE THREE THINGS THAT YOU KNOW YOU SHOULD DO BUT HAVE BEEN PUTTING OFF? DO THEM AND CONGRATULATE YOURSELF FOR YOUR SELF-DISCIPLINE!

Notes

KEEP GOING AND GROWING

I continue learning. I read books and listen to the right people.
I earn new skills and attend classes. I study sustainable gardening and the new digital economy.
I broaden my mindset, skills and Always Invest In my Education.

If I accept myself as I am, how do I bring the change?

What is one new thing I want to try today?

How would I describe my personal growth path?

KEEP GOING AND GROWING

I continue learning. I read books and listen to the right people.
I earn new skills and attend classes. I study sustainable gardening and the new digital economy.
I broaden my mindset, skills and Always Invest In my Education.

If I accept myself as I am, how do I bring the change?

What is one new thing I want to try today?

How would I describe my personal growth path?

Notes

LEARN SOMETHING NEW

FIVE NEW SKILLS TO LEARN

What skills can I build to facilitate gaining power?

LEARN SOMETHING NEW

Do I present myself as someone that is powerful? How can I enhance my image?

Five future adventures

LEARN SOMETHING NEW

FIVE OBSTACLES TO REMOVE

FIVE ISSUES TO RESOLVE

Notes

Part 6

SMART Goal Setting

GOALS JOURNAL

First, consider what you want to achieve, and then commit to it. Set SMART (specific, measureable, attainable, relevant and time-bound) goals that motivate you and write them down to make them feel tangible. Then plan the steps you must take to realize your goal, and cross off each one as you work through them.

A GOAL WITHOUT A PLAN IS JUST A WISH.

GOAL SETTING IS A POWERFUL PROCESS FOR THINKING ABOUT YOUR IDEAL FUTURE, AND FOR MOTIVATING YOURSELF TO TURN YOUR VISION OF THIS FUTURE INTO REALITY.

GOALS JOURNAL

WHY DO I WANT TO ACHIEVE MY GOALS?

HOW CAN I ACHIEVE THEM?

REMINDER

NOTE

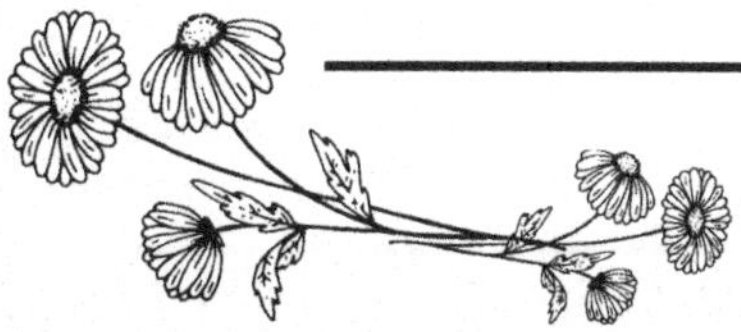

SMART Goal Setting Journal

1

Write down your goal in as few words as possible.

My goal is to:

SMART Goal Setting Journal

Make your goal detailed and SPECIFIC.
Answer who/what/where/how/when.

2

How will you reach this goal?
List at least 3 action steps you'll take (be specific):

SMART Goal Setting Journal

3 Make your goal MEASURABLE. Add details, measurements and tracking details.

I will measure/track my goal by using the following numbers or methods:

I will know I've reached my goal when

SMART Goal Setting Journal

MAKE YOUR GOAL ATTAINABLE. WHAT ADDITIONAL RESOURCES DO YOU NEED FOR SUCCESS?

4

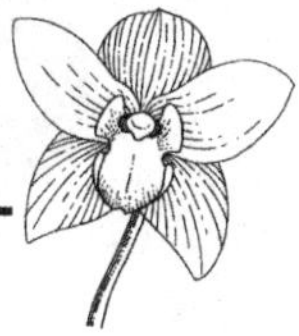

ITEMS I NEED TO ACHIEVE THIS GOAL:

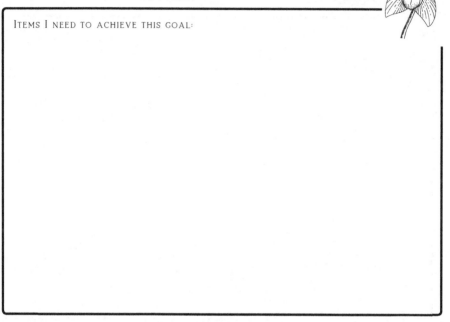

HOW I'LL FIND THE TIME:

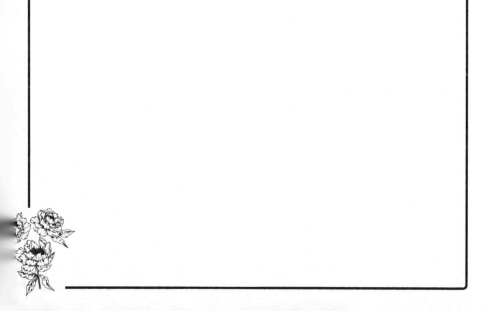

SMART Goal Setting Journal

4 Make your goal ATTAINABLE. What additional resources do you need for success?

Things I need to learn more about:

People I can talk to for support:

SMART Goal Setting Journal

MAKE YOUR GOAL RELEVANT. LIST WHY YOU WANT TO REACH THIS GOAL:

5

SMART Goal Setting Journal

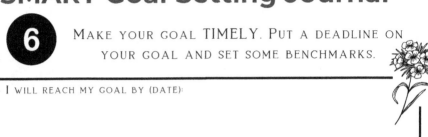

6 MAKE YOUR GOAL TIMELY. PUT A DEADLINE ON YOUR GOAL AND SET SOME BENCHMARKS.

I WILL REACH MY GOAL BY (DATE):

MY HALFWAY MEASUREMENT WILL BE ON...

ADDITIONAL DATES AND MILESTONES I'LL AIM FOR:

My Notes

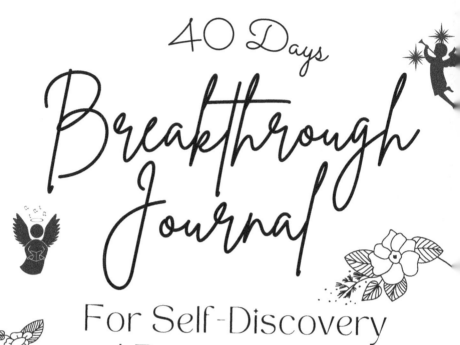

40 Days Breakthrough Journal

For Self-Discovery and Personal Growth

ONE WORLD MANY STORIES

My 45 Days Overview

MONTH :

YEAR :

DREAM BIG AND CREATE YOUR OWN STORY

DAY 1	DAY 2	DAY 3	DAY 4
DAY 5	DAY 6	DAY 7	DAY 8
DAY 9	DAY 10	DAY 11	DAY 12
DAY 13	DAY 14	DAY 15	DAY 16
DAY 17	DAY 18	DAY 19	DAY 20
DAY 21	DAY 22	DAY 23	DAY 24

All Things are possible if you believe

TO DO LIST

Day 25 ☐	Day 26 ☐	Day 27 ☐
Day 28 ☐	Day 29 ☐	Day 30 ☐
Day 31 ☐	Day 32 ☐	Day 33 ☐
Day 34 ☐	Day 35 ☐	Day 36 ☐
Day 37 ☐	Day 38 ☐	Day 39 ☐
Day 40 ☐	Bonus ☐	Bonus ☐

Notes

My Habits

- ☆
- ☆
- ☆
- ☆
- ☆

DAY 1

Daily Journal

DATE :

TODAY I'M GRATEFUL FOR

MY PRIORITIES

☆ GOALS

TO DO LIST

☐ EDUCATION

☐ SKILLS

☐ TRAVELING

☐ MIND/BODY

☐ SPIRITUALITY

DAILY CHECK-UP

MY MOOD TODAY

1 2 3 4 5 6 7 8 9 10

THREE WORDS THAT DESCRIBE TODAY?

MY NEW HABITS

ACTIVITIES

NOTE:

Who am I?

Answer with one-word nouns or short sentences. Keep asking yourself the same question over and over. Continue to write different answers in each space.

My Core Values	Rank

Notes

DAY 2

Daily Journal

DATE :

TODAY I'M GRATEFUL FOR

MY PRIORITIES

☆ GOALS

TO DO LIST

☐ EDUCATION

☐ SKILLS

☐ TRAVELING

☐ MIND/BODY

☐ SPIRITUALITY

DAILY CHECK-UP

MY MOOD TODAY

1 2 3 4 5 6 7 8 9 10

THREE WORDS THAT DESCRIBE TODAY?

MY NEW HABITS

ACTIVITIES

NOTE:

What I Want?

Things I Want to Have in Life

CREATE A LIST OF MATERIAL THINGS THAT YOU WOULD LIKE TO HAVE IN LIFE. WRITE IT DOWN EVEN IF YOU THINK IT COULD NEVER HAPPEN.

Things I Want to Do in Life

CREATE A LIST OF 10 THINGS YOU WANT TO DO IN YOUR LIFE BEFORE YOU DIE. DO YOU WANT TO LEARN HOW TO DO SOMETHING? BE CREATIVE. WRITE IT DOWN EVEN IF YOU THINK IT COULD NEVER HAPPEN.

DAY 3

Daily Journal

DATE :

TODAY I'M GRATEFUL FOR	MY PRIORITIES

☆ GOALS

TO DO LIST	DAILY CHECK-UP
☐ EDUCATION	MY MOOD TODAY 1 2 3 4 5 6 7 8 9 10 THREE WORDS THAT DESCRIBE TODAY?
☐ SKILLS	MY NEW HABITS
☐ TRAVELING	
☐ MIND/BODY	ACTIVITIES
☐ SPIRITUALITY	NOTE:

Develop a Present Moment Mindset

WHAT ARE THE ADVANTAGES I WOULD ENJOY IF I COULD STAY FOCUSED ON THE PRESENT?

Notes

DAY 4

Daily Journal

DATE :

TODAY I'M GRATEFUL FOR

MY PRIORITIES

☆ GOALS

TO DO LIST

☐ EDUCATION

☐ SKILLS

☐ TRAVELING

☐ MIND/BODY

☐ SPIRITUALITY

DAILY CHECK-UP

MY MOOD TODAY

1 2 3 4 5 6 7 8 9 10

THREE WORDS THAT DESCRIBE TODAY?

MY NEW HABITS

ACTIVITIES

NOTE:

Personal growth and life goals

DO YOUR GOALS TRULY REFLECT YOUR DESIRES? OR DO THEY REFLECT WHAT SOMEONE ELSE (A PARENT, PARTNER, FRIEND, ETC.) WANTS FOR YOU?

WHAT HELPS YOU STAY FOCUSED AND MOTIVATED WHEN YOU FEEL DISCOURAGED?

WHAT DO YOU LOOK FORWARD TO MOST IN THE FUTURE?

DAY 5

Daily Journal

DATE :

TODAY I'M GRATEFUL FOR	MY PRIORITIES

☆ GOALS

TO DO LIST

☐ EDUCATION

☐ SKILLS

☐ TRAVELING

☐ MIND/BODY

☐ SPIRITUALITY

DAILY CHECK-UP

MY MOOD TODAY

1 2 3 4 5 6 7 8 9 10

THREE WORDS THAT DESCRIBE TODAY?

MY NEW HABITS

ACTIVITIES

NOTE:

WHAT "SUCCESS" MEANS TO ME

NOTES:

Daily Journal

DAY 6

DATE :

TODAY I'M GRATEFUL FOR

MY PRIORITIES

☆ GOALS

TO DO LIST

☐ EDUCATION

☐ SKILLS

☐ TRAVELING

☐ MIND/BODY

☐ SPIRITUALITY

DAILY CHECK-UP

MY MOOD TODAY

1 2 3 4 5 6 7 8 9 10

THREE WORDS THAT DESCRIBE TODAY?

MY NEW HABITS

ACTIVITIES

NOTE:

WHAT SKILL DO I NEED TO WORK IN MY PASSION?

CREATE AND SHARE AMAZING MIND MAPS!

DAY 7

Daily Journal

DATE :

TODAY I'M GRATEFUL FOR

MY PRIORITIES

☆ GOALS

TO DO LIST

EDUCATION

SKILLS

TRAVELING

MIND/BODY

SPIRITUALITY

DAILY CHECK-UP

MY MOOD TODAY

1 2 3 4 5 6 7 8 9 10

THREE WORDS THAT DESCRIBE TODAY?

MY NEW HABITS

ACTIVITIES

NOTE:

What are 5 things that make me happy? And What can I do to improve the world?

Daily Journal

DAY 8

DATE :

TODAY I'M GRATEFUL FOR

MY PRIORITIES

☆ GOALS

TO DO LIST

- [ ]
- [ ]
- [ ]
- [ ]
- [ ]
- [ ]

WHAT TYPE OF PERSON AM I TODAY?

DESCRIBE THE PERSON I WANT TO BECOME!

DAILY CHECK-UP

MY MOOD TODAY

1 2 3 4 5 6 7 8 9 10

THREE WORDS THAT DESCRIBE TODAY?

MY NEW HABITS

1
2
3
4
5

ACTIVITIES

NOTE:

7 Quick facts about me?

NOTES:

DAY 9

Daily Journal

DATE :

TODAY I'M GRATEFUL FOR

MY PRIORITIES

☆ GOALS

TO DO LIST

- [ ]
- [ ]
- [ ]
- [ ]
- [ ]
- [ ]

WHAT TYPE OF PERSON AM I TODAY?

DESCRIBE THE PERSON I WANT TO BECOME!

DAILY CHECK-UP

MY MOOD TODAY

1 2 3 4 5 6 7 8 9 10

THREE WORDS THAT DESCRIBE TODAY?

MY NEW HABITS

1
2
3
4
5

ACTIVITIES

NOTE:

10-Minute Reflection Exercises

IF I CAN ELIMINATE ONE THING FROM MY LIFE TO ?

IF I COULD CHANGE ONE THING ABOUT THE WORLD WHAT WOULD IT BE?

WHAT IS THE BEST WAY TO GET STARTED?. BE SPECIFIC AND VISUALIZE IT.

DAY 10

Daily Journal

DATE :

TODAY I'M GRATEFUL FOR

MY PRIORITIES

☆ GOALS

TO DO LIST

- [ ]
- [ ]
- [ ]
- [ ]
- [ ]
- [ ]

WHAT TYPE OF PERSON AM I TODAY?

DESCRIBE THE PERSON I WANT TO BECOME!

DAILY CHECK-UP

MY MOOD TODAY

1 2 3 4 5 6 7 8 9 10

THREE WORDS THAT DESCRIBE TODAY?

MY NEW HABITS

1
2
3
4
5

ACTIVITIES

NOTE:

Sharing Ideas

With interesting questions, you can spark some great ideas!
Share your thoughts with someone and listen to their thoughts, too.

What makes you feel fulfilled?

What talent can you do with ease?

How do You define intentional living?

What goals do I want to achieve this quarter?

What helps you slow down and feel more present?

How can you step outside your comfort zone to grow?

NOTES :

DAY 11

Daily Journal

DATE :

TODAY I'M GRATEFUL FOR

MY PRIORITIES

☆ GOALS

TO DO LIST

- [ ]
- [ ]
- [ ]
- [ ]
- [ ]
- [ ]

DAILY CHECK-UP

MY MOOD TODAY

1 2 3 4 5 6 7 8 9 10

THREE WORDS THAT DESCRIBE TODAY?

MY NEW HABITS

1
2
3
4
5

ACTIVITIES

DAILY AFFIRMATIONS

STRONG FOCUS ON WHAT I WANT

NOTE:

In order to plan your ideal life, you should start by describing the kind of life you want to have in the future. What will your typical day consist of?

DAY 12

Daily Journal

DATE :

TODAY I'M GRATEFUL FOR

MY PRIORITIES

☆ GOALS

TO DO LIST

- [ ]
- [ ]
- [ ]
- [ ]
- [ ]
- [ ]

DAILY AFFIRMATIONS

STRONG FOCUS ON WHAT I WANT

DAILY CHECK-UP

MY MOOD TODAY

1 2 3 4 5 6 7 8 9 10

THREE WORDS THAT DESCRIBE TODAY?

MY NEW HABITS

1
2
3
4
5

ACTIVITIES

NOTE:

Be Clear About Your Decisions

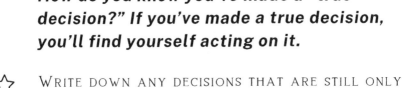

How do you know you've made a "true decision?" If you've made a true decision, you'll find yourself acting on it.

☆ WRITE DOWN ANY DECISIONS THAT ARE STILL ONLY DREAMS - SOMETHING I'LL DO "SOMEDAY."

☆ HOW CAN I EMPOWER THESE DECISIONS?

Daily Journal

DAY 13

DATE :

TODAY I'M GRATEFUL FOR

MY PRIORITIES

☆ GOALS

TO DO LIST

- [ ]
- [ ]
- [ ]
- [ ]
- [ ]
- [ ]

DAILY AFFIRMATIONS

STRONG FOCUS ON WHAT I WANT

DAILY CHECK-UP

MY MOOD TODAY

1 2 3 4 5 6 7 8 9 10

THREE WORDS THAT DESCRIBE TODAY?

MY NEW HABITS

1
2
3
4
5

ACTIVITIES

NOTE:

The Three Decisions That Will Shape Your Life

WHAT IS THE PRIMARY FOCUS OF MY LIFE?

Decide how the situations you find yourself in today affect your present and future.

SITUATION 1:

EFFECT ON THE PRESENT MOMENT:

POSSIBLE EFFECT ON MY FUTURE:

SITUATION 2:

EFFECT ON THE PRESENT MOMENT:

POSSIBLE EFFECT ON MY FUTURE:

AND NOW FOR THE MOST IMPORTANT DECISION: LOOKING AT MY CURRENT SITUATION, WHAT SHOULD I DO NOW? THE QUICKER AND MORE DECISIVE THE DECISION, THE GREATER THE IMPACT ON MY LIFE.

NOTES

Daily Journal

DAY 14

DATE :

TODAY I'M GRATEFUL FOR

MY PRIORITIES

☆ GOALS

TO DO LIST

- [ ]
- [ ]
- [ ]
- [ ]
- [ ]
- [ ]

DAILY AFFIRMATIONS

STRONG FOCUS ON WHAT I WANT

DAILY CHECK-UP

MY MOOD TODAY

1 2 3 4 5 6 7 8 9 10

THREE WORDS THAT DESCRIBE TODAY?

MY NEW HABITS

1
2
3
4
5

ACTIVITIES

NOTE:

TRANSFORMING MYSELF

TRANSFORMATION IS NOT A LONG PROCESS

It happens in an instant, provided that you've been working towards it. Do you have a stunning intention to change?

Ask yourself What do I really want to change now? Be specific and visualize it.

NOW USE THE PAIN AND PLEASURE PRINCIPLES BY ANSWERING THE QUESTIONS BELOW

What will this cost me if I don't change?

WHAT HAS IT ALREADY COST ME PHYSICALLY, SPIRITUALLY, MENTALLY, CAREER-WISE, AND IN MY RELATIONSHIPS?

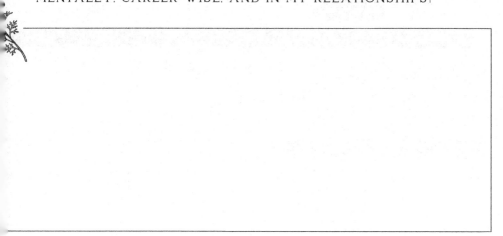

HOW HAS IT AFFECTED OUR PEOPLE ?

HOW WILL THIS CHANGE MAKE OUR WORLD FEEL?

15-Days Overview

DAY 15

DATE :

MOOD METER

MOTIVATION METER

NEW HABITS

1 2 3 4 5 6 7 8 9 10 11 12

HABITS OVERVIEW

PRODUCTIVITY

TO DO LIST:

PRIORITIES

POP OF

POSITIVITY

MY MANTRA

SHARE A POP

HOW TO QUIET MY MIND

A SMALL ACHIEVEMENT

WHAT IS THE MOST IMPORTANT THING I HAVE LEARNED ABOUT MYSELF DURING MY 15 DAYS JOURNEY?

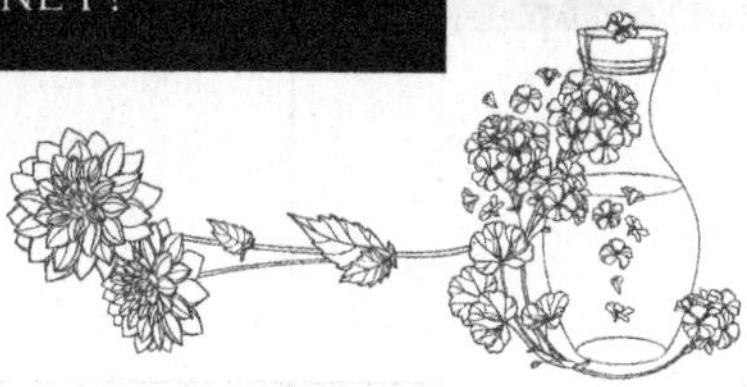

I'm grateful for

DAY 16

Daily Journal

DATE

TODAY I'M GRATEFUL FOR

MY PRIORITIES

☆ GOALS

TO DO LIST

- [ ]
- [ ]
- [ ]
- [ ]
- [ ]
- [ ]

STRONG FOCUS ON WHAT I WANT

WAYS TO BE KIND TO OTHERS

DAILY CHECK-UP

MY MOOD TODAY

1 2 3 4 5 6 7 8 9 10

WHY DO I FEEL THIS WAY?

EDUCATION/SKILL

1
2
3
4
5

ACTIVITIES/TRY SOMETHING NEW

NOTE:

My Soul Connection

DATE :

THINGS I CAN DO WHEN I AM SAD

THINGS I CAN DO WHEN I AM BORED

I AM LOOKING FORWARD TO

MY FAVORITE MOVIES

SPECIAL PAMPERING CHECKLIST

MY FAVORITE SHOWS

MY FAVORITE BOOKS

MY FAVORITE SONGS

NOTES

DAY 17

Daily Journal

DATE:

TODAY I'M GRATEFUL FOR

MY PRIORITIES

☆ GOALS

TO DO LIST

- [ ]
- [ ]
- [ ]
- [ ]
- [ ]
- [ ]

STRONG FOCUS ON WHAT I WANT

WAYS TO BE KIND TO OTHERS

DAILY CHECK-UP

MY MOOD TODAY

1 2 3 4 5 6 7 8 9 10

WHY DO I FEEL THIS WAY?

EDUCATION/SKILL

1
2
3
4
5

ACTIVITIES/TRY SOMETHING NEW

NOTE:

HOW DID YOU FEEL ABOUT WORKING WITH OTHERS AS A CHILD AND AS A TEEN? DID YOU LIKE BEING A LEADER, WORKING ALONE, WORKING WITH SMALL OR LARGE GROUPS? WHAT ROLE DID YOU TAKE? WHAT ROLE DID YOU WANT TO TAKE?

DO YOU THINK YOUR IDEAL CAREER IS OUT OF REACH OR IMPOSSIBLE? AND WRITE 5 THINGS YOU DID TO MAKE YOUR DREAM COME TRUE

DAY 18

Daily Journal

DATE

TODAY I'M GRATEFUL FOR

MY PRIORITIES

GOALS

TO DO LIST

- [ ]
- [ ]
- [ ]
- [ ]
- [ ]
- [ ]

STRONG FOCUS ON WHAT I WANT

WAYS TO BE KIND TO OTHERS

DAILY CHECK-UP

MY MOOD TODAY

1 2 3 4 5 6 7 8 9 10

WHY DO I FEEL THIS WAY?

EDUCATION/SKILL

1
2
3
4
5

ACTIVITIES/TRY SOMETHING NEW

NOTE:

Beyond TOMORROW

WHAT STEPS WILL I TAKE OUTSIDE MY COMFORT ZONE TO ACHIEVE THESE GOALS?

WHO CAN I TALK TO THAT HAS BEEN WHERE I AM TRYING TO GO?

1

2

WHAT DO I NEED TO LEARN TODAY THAT WILL HELP WITH MY GOAL?

WHAT THING CAN I LEARN MORE ABOUT TO MAKE ME FEEL MORE CONFIDENT IN MY CAREER/IDEAL CAREER?

DAY 19

Daily Journal

DATE :

TODAY I'M GRATEFUL FOR

MY PRIORITIES

☆ GOALS

TO DO LIST

- [ ]
- [ ]
- [ ]
- [ ]
- [ ]
- [ ]

DAILY CHECK-UP

MY MOOD TODAY

1 2 3 4 5 6 7 8 9 10

WHY DO I FEEL THIS WAY?

EDUCATION/SKILL

1
2
3
4
5

ACTIVITIES/TRY SOMETHING NEW

NOTE:

STRONG FOCUS ON WHAT I WANT

WAYS TO BE KIND TO OTHERS

WHAT WILL MY LIFE LOOK LIKE IN

3 YEARS?

5 YEARS?

10 YEARS?

CREATE A VISION BOARD

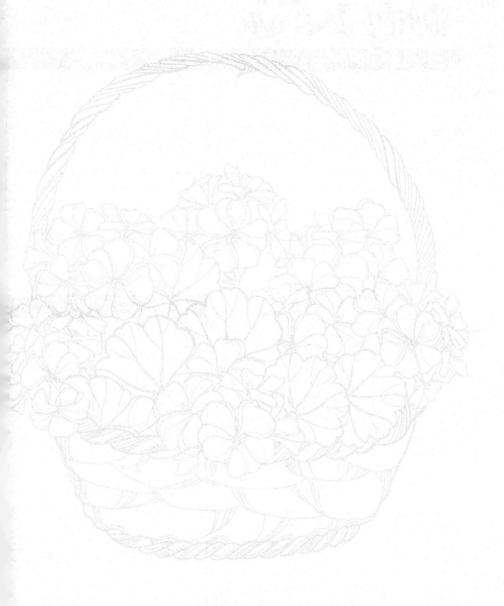

DAY 20

Daily Journal

DATE:

TODAY I'M GRATEFUL FOR

MY PRIORITIES

☆ GOALS

TO DO LIST

☐ ____________________

☐ ____________________

☐ ____________________

☐ ____________________

☐ ____________________

☐

STRONG FOCUS ON WHAT I WANT

WAYS TO BE KIND TO OTHERS

DAILY CHECK-UP

MY MOOD TODAY

1 2 3 4 5 6 7 8 9 10

WHY DO I FEEL THIS WAY?

EDUCATION/SKILL

1

2

3

4

5

ACTIVITIES/TRY SOMETHING NEW

NOTE:

List my amazing support communities here:

What are my favorite quotes that resonate with me?

DAY 21

Daily Journal

DATE

TODAY I'M GRATEFUL FOR

MY PRIORITIES

☆ GOALS

TO DO LIST

- [ ]
- [ ]
- [ ]
- [ ]
- [ ]
- [ ]

STRONG FOCUS ON WHAT I WANT

WAYS TO BE KIND TO OTHERS

DAILY CHECK-UP

MY MOOD TODAY

1 2 3 4 5 6 7 8 9 10

WHY DO I FEEL THIS WAY?

EDUCATION/SKILL

1
2
3
4
5

ACTIVITIES/TRY SOMETHING NEW

NOTE:

DO I STRIVE TO DEVELOP MY "Talents"?

HOW?

HOW DO I AFFECT OTHERS? DO I ENCOURAGE THEM OR DISCOURAGE THEM?

DAY 22

Daily Journal

DATE :

TODAY I'M GRATEFUL FOR

MY PRIORITIES

☆ GOALS

TO DO LIST

- [ ]
- [ ]
- [ ]
- [ ]
- [ ]
- [ ]

WHAT CAN I DO TODAY TO MOVE CLOSER TOWARD MY GOALS?

WAYS TO BE KIND TO OTHERS

DAILY CHECK-UP

MY MOOD TODAY

1 2 3 4 5 6 7 8 9 10

WHY DO I FEEL THIS WAY?

EDUCATION/SKILL

1
2
3
4
5

ACTIVITIES/TRY SOMETHING NEW

NOTE:

Write Why Being Strong Matters

Own your POWER

DOES YOUR DESIRE TO SUCCEED RUN DEEPER THAN YOUR FEAR OF FAILURE?

Write Why Being Strong Matters

ARE YOU READY TO DIG DEEP AND WRITE YOUR OWN SUCCESS STORY? JOT DOWN SOME AMAZING IDEAS...

DAY 23

Daily Journal

DATE :

TODAY I'M GRATEFUL FOR

MY PRIORITIES

☆ GOALS

TO DO LIST

- [ ] ______
- [ ] ______
- [ ] ______
- [ ] ______
- [ ] ______
- [ ] ______

WHAT CAN I DO TODAY TO MOVE CLOSER TOWARD MY GOALS?

WAYS TO BE KIND TO OTHERS

DAILY CHECK-UP

MY MOOD TODAY

1 2 3 4 5 6 7 8 9 10

WHY DO I FEEL THIS WAY?

EDUCATION/SKILL

1
2
3
4
5

ACTIVITIES/TRY SOMETHING NEW

NOTE:

OVERCOMING WRITER'S BLOCK

Mindfulness Wheel

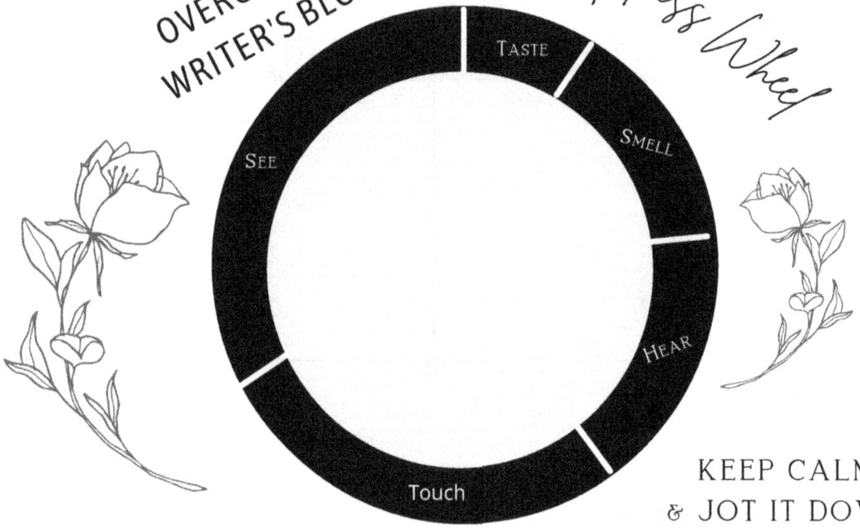

KEEP CALM
& JOT IT DOWN

5 THINGS I CAN SEE

1 ____________________
2 ____________________
3 ____________________
4 ____________________
5 ____________________

4 THINGS I CAN TOUCH

1 ____________________
2 ____________________
3 ____________________
4 ____________________

3 THINGS I CAN HEAR

1 ____________________
2 ____________________
3 ____________________

2 THINGS I CAN SMELL

1 ____________________
2 ____________________

2 THINGS I CAN TASTE

1 ____________________

NOTES:

Soul JOURNEY

Nature Connection

INTENTIONS

Ideas to Connect with Nature

- Go For a Drive with the windows down
- meditate
-
-
-
-

THINGS I DID TO CONNECT WITH NATURE THIS DAY

INSPIRATION: ....

NOTE:

DAY 24

Daily Journal

DATE :

TODAY I'M GRATEFUL FOR

MY PRIORITIES

☆ GOALS

TO DO LIST

- [ ]
- [ ]
- [ ]
- [ ]
- [ ]
- [ ]

WHAT CAN I DO TODAY TO MOVE CLOSER TOWARD MY GOALS?

WAYS TO BE KIND TO OTHERS

DAILY CHECK-UP

MY MOOD TODAY

1 2 3 4 5 6 7 8 9 10

WHY DO I FEEL THIS WAY?

EDUCATION/SKILL

1
2
3
4
5

ACTIVITIES/TRY SOMETHING NEW

NOTE:

SELF-REFLECTION QUESTIONS

JOURNAL EXERCISE

HOW DOES ACCEPTING MYSELF AS I AM HELP ME TO MAKE POSITIVE CHANGES?

SELF-REFLECTION QUESTIONS

JOURNAL EXERCISE

MY NEW THING FOR TODAY PROJECT

HOW WOULD I DESCRIBE MY PERSONAL GROWTH PATH?

DAY 25

Daily Journal

DATE :

TODAY I'M GRATEFUL FOR

MY PRIORITIES

☆ GOALS

TO DO LIST

- [ ]
- [ ]
- [ ]
- [ ]
- [ ]
- [ ]

WHAT CAN I DO TODAY TO MOVE CLOSER TOWARD MY GOALS?

WAYS TO BE KIND TO OTHERS

DAILY CHECK-UP

MY MOOD TODAY

1 2 3 4 5 6 7 8 9 10

WHY DO I FEEL THIS WAY?

EDUCATION/SKILL

1
2
3
4
5

ACTIVITIES/TRY SOMETHING NEW

NOTE:

3-step guide to mindful gratitude

1 START BY OBSERVING. HOW MANY THANK YOU'S DID I SAY FOR THIS WEEK? HOW AM I FEELING WHEN YOU EXPRESS THANKS?

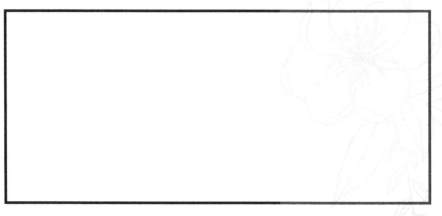

2 3 THINGS I AM DOING WELL CURRENTLY

3 My Powerful Quotes

Harmony Life

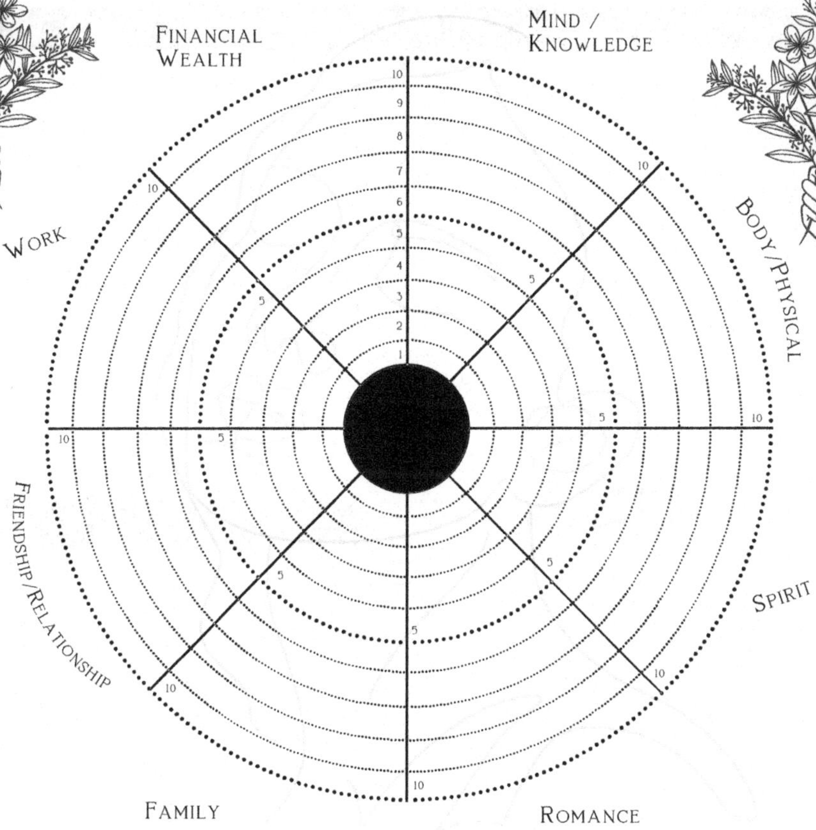

Milestones:

Notes

DAY 26

Daily Journal

DATE :

TODAY I'M GRATEFUL FOR

MY PRIORITIES

☆ GOALS

TO DO LIST

- [ ]
- [ ]
- [ ]
- [ ]
- [ ]
- [ ]

WHAT CAN I DO TODAY TO MOVE CLOSER TOWARD MY GOALS?

WAYS TO BE KIND TO OTHERS

DAILY CHECK-UP

MY MOOD TODAY

1 2 3 4 5 6 7 8 9 10

WHY DO I FEEL THIS WAY?

EDUCATION/SKILL

1
2
3
4
5

ACTIVITIES/TRY SOMETHING NEW

NOTE:

Observing a new world

It's time to explore!

Search for a topic you're interested in on Google/Facebook and look for the questions Google/Facebook suggests. Choose 1 and write an article on this topic. You may have to try a ton of different searches to see suggested questions.

DAY 27

Daily Journal

DATE :

TODAY I'M GRATEFUL FOR

MY PRIORITIES

☆ GOALS

TO DO LIST

- [ ]
- [ ]
- [ ]
- [ ]
- [ ]
- [ ]

WHAT CAN I DO TODAY TO MOVE CLOSER TOWARD MY GOALS?

WAYS TO BE KIND TO OTHERS

DAILY CHECK-UP

MY MOOD TODAY

1 2 3 4 5 6 7 8 9 10

WHY DO I FEEL THIS WAY?

EDUCATION/SKILL

1
2
3
4
5

ACTIVITIES/TRY SOMETHING NEW

NOTE:

ONLINE BUSINESS IDEAS YOU CAN START TODAY

WRITE A SHORT AUTOBIOGRAPHY OF YOUR LIFE IN THE FORM OF AN INTERVIEW, WHERE PARAGRAPHS ALTERNATE BETWEEN QUESTION AND ANSWER.

DAY 28

Daily Journal

DATE :

TODAY I'M GRATEFUL FOR

MY PRIORITIES

☆ GOALS

TO DO LIST

☐ ____

☐ ____

☐ ____

☐ ____

☐ ____

☐ ____

WHAT CAN I DO TODAY TO MOVE CLOSER TOWARD MY GOALS?

MY NEW HABITS

DAILY CHECK-UP

MY MOOD TODAY

1 2 3 4 5 6 7 8 9 10

WHY DO I FEEL THIS WAY?

EDUCATION/SKILL

1
2
3
4
5

ACTIVITIES/TRY SOMETHING NEW

NOTE:

FIND 3-5 BOOKS OR WEBSITES ABOUT THINGS YOU'RE INTERESTED IN, AND JOURNAL 5 TOP BITS ABOUT EACH SITE/AUTHOR/EXPERT SUCH AS THE GOAL OF THE BOOK/SITE, HOW TO CHANGE THE WORLD, WHAT PRODUCTS OR SERVICES IT OFFERS, RELATED PRODUCTS/PEOPLE, ETC.

DAY 29

Daily Journal

DATE :

TODAY I'M GRATEFUL FOR

MY PRIORITIES

☆ GOALS

TO DO LIST

- [ ]
- [ ]
- [ ]
- [ ]
- [ ]
- [ ]

WHAT CAN I DO TODAY TO MOVE CLOSER TOWARD MY GOALS?

MY NEW HABITS

DAILY CHECK-UP

MY MOOD TODAY

1 2 3 4 5 6 7 8 9 10

WHY DO I FEEL THIS WAY?

EDUCATION/SKILL

1
2
3
4
5

ACTIVITIES/TRY SOMETHING NEW

NOTE:

I LOVE MYSELF

WRITE DOWN 3 ACTIONS YOU CAN TAKE EACH DAY TOWARDS DISCOVERING YOUR PASSION AND CREATING YOUR OWN SUCCESS.

DAY 30

Daily Journal

DATE :

TODAY I'M GRATEFUL FOR

MY PRIORITIES

Goals

TO DO LIST

- [ ]
- [ ]
- [ ]
- [ ]
- [ ]
- [ ]

What can I do today to move closer toward my goals?

My New Habits

DAILY CHECK-UP

MY MOOD TODAY

1 2 3 4 5 6 7 8 9 10

WHY DO I FEEL THIS WAY?

Education/skill

1
2
3
4
5

Activities/try something new

Note:

The Inner World Adventure

Find happiness from within

1. Describe what love means to you in detail

2. What element do you consider to be YOU? Write about why. (Earth, Air, Fire, Water)

3. Physically, how do you feel right now?

DAY 31

Daily Journal

DATE :

TODAY I'M GRATEFUL FOR

MY PRIORITIES

GOALS

TO DO LIST

- [ ]
- [ ]
- [ ]
- [ ]
- [ ]
- [ ]

WHAT CAN I DO TODAY TO MOVE CLOSER TOWARD MY GOALS?

MY NEW HABITS

DAILY CHECK-UP

MY MOOD TODAY

1 2 3 4 5 6 7 8 9 10

WHY DO I FEEL THIS WAY?

EDUCATION/SKILL

1
2
3
4
5

ACTIVITIES/TRY SOMETHING NEW

NOTE:

List your top 5 companies to work for if you could work for anyone and give us some reason why you chose those companies.

DAY 32

Daily Journal

DATE :

TODAY I'M GRATEFUL FOR

MY PRIORITIES

☆ GOALS

TO DO LIST

- [ ]
- [ ]
- [ ]
- [ ]
- [ ]
- [ ]

WHAT CAN I DO TODAY TO MOVE CLOSER TOWARD MY GOALS?

MY NEW HABITS

DAILY CHECK-UP

MY MOOD TODAY

1 2 3 4 5 6 7 8 9 10

WHY DO I FEEL THIS WAY?

EDUCATION/SKILL

1
2
3
4
5

ACTIVITIES/TRY SOMETHING NEW

NOTE:

Reflection Writing Exercise

10 POSITIVE ANSWERS YOU'D LIKE TO SHARE WITH OTHERS ABOUT DISCOVERING YOUR PASSION.

DAY 33

Daily Journal

DATE :

TODAY I'M GRATEFUL FOR

MY PRIORITIES

☆ 3 THINGS YOU ARE DOING WELL CURRENTLY

TO DO LIST

- [ ]
- [ ]
- [ ]
- [ ]
- [ ]
- [ ]

DID YOU DO SOMETHING NICE TO SOMEONE TODAY? WRITE ABOUT IT.

CAN YOU DO BETTER TOMORROW? HOW?

DAILY CHECK-UP

MY MOOD TODAY

1 2 3 4 5 6 7 8 9 10

WHY DO I FEEL THIS WAY?

EDUCATION/SKILL

1
2
3
4
5

MY NEW HABITS

NOTE:

THE WONDERFUL DAY TO REMEMBER

WRITE A LIST OF 7 THINGS YOU WANT TO REMEMBER DURING DIFFICULT TIMES. (USE THIS LATER IF YOU'RE FEELING DOWN).

DAY 34

Daily Journal

DATE :

TODAY I'M GRATEFUL FOR

MY PRIORITIES

☆ 3 THINGS YOU ARE DOING WELL CURRENTLY

TO DO LIST

- [ ] ______
- [ ] ______
- [ ] ______
- [ ] ______
- [ ] ______
- [ ]

DID YOU DO SOMETHING NICE TO SOMEONE TODAY? WRITE ABOUT IT.

CAN YOU DO BETTER TOMORROW? HOW?

DAILY CHECK-UP

MY MOOD TODAY

1 2 3 4 5 6 7 8 9 10

WHY DO I FEEL THIS WAY?

EDUCATION/SKILL

1
2
3
4
5

MY NEW HABITS

NOTE:

EXPOSITORY WRITING

Creating a Perfect Idea

How are you influencing the world? Write about the improvements and create a plan to accomplish each one.

DAY 35

Daily Journal

DATE :

TODAY I'M GRATEFUL FOR

MY PRIORITIES

☆ 3 THINGS YOU ARE DOING WELL CURRENTLY

TO DO LIST

- [ ]
- [ ]
- [ ]
- [ ]
- [ ]
- [ ]

DID YOU DO SOMETHING NICE TO SOMEONE TODAY? WRITE ABOUT IT.

CAN YOU DO BETTER TOMORROW? HOW?

DAILY CHECK-UP

MY MOOD TODAY

1 2 3 4 5 6 7 8 9 10

WHY DO I FEEL THIS WAY?

EDUCATION/SKILL

1
2
3
4
5

MY NEW HABITS

NOTE:

A Life-Changing Situation

WHAT DON'T YOU KNOW THAT YOU DON'T KNOW?

BREAK THOSE CHAINS THAT BIND YOU AND SET YOURSELF FREE!

DAY 36

Daily Journal

DATE :

TODAY I'M GRATEFUL FOR

MY PRIORITIES

3 THINGS YOU ARE DOING WELL CURRENTLY

TO DO LIST

- [ ]
- [ ]
- [ ]
- [ ]
- [ ]
- [ ]

DID YOU DO SOMETHING NICE TO SOMEONE TODAY? WRITE ABOUT IT.

CAN YOU DO BETTER TOMORROW? HOW?

DAILY CHECK-UP

MY MOOD TODAY

1 2 3 4 5 6 7 8 9 10

WHY DO I FEEL THIS WAY?

EDUCATION/SKILL

1
2
3
4
5

MY NEW HABITS

NOTE:

A WRITING PROMPT EXERCISE

My Journal for self-discovery and self-reflection

WHAT'S THE MOST IMPORTANT LESSON I'VE LEARNED SO FAR IN MY JOURNEY? AM I LIVING THAT LESSON?

DAY 37

Daily Journal

DATE :

TODAY I'M GRATEFUL FOR	MY PRIORITIES

☆ 3 THINGS YOU ARE DOING WELL CURRENTLY

TO DO LIST

- [ ]
- [ ]
- [ ]
- [ ]
- [ ]
- [ ]

DID YOU DO SOMETHING NICE TO SOMEONE TODAY? WRITE ABOUT IT.

CAN YOU DO BETTER TOMORROW? HOW?

DAILY CHECK-UP

MY MOOD TODAY

1 2 3 4 5 6 7 8 9 10

WHY DO I FEEL THIS WAY?

EDUCATION/SKILL

1
2
3
4
5

MY NEW HABITS

NOTE:

MY SELF-CARE REFLECTION

Write about your reflections about a specific experience.

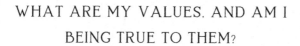

WHAT ARE MY VALUES, AND AM I BEING TRUE TO THEM?

DAY 38

Daily Journal

DATE :

TODAY I'M GRATEFUL FOR

MY PRIORITIES

☆ 3 THINGS YOU ARE DOING WELL CURRENTLY

TO DO LIST

- [ ]
- [ ]
- [ ]
- [ ]
- [ ]
- [ ]

DID YOU DO SOMETHING NICE TO SOMEONE TODAY? WRITE ABOUT IT.

CAN YOU DO BETTER TOMORROW? HOW?

DAILY CHECK-UP

MY MOOD TODAY

1 2 3 4 5 6 7 8 9 10

WHY DO I FEEL THIS WAY?

EDUCATION/SKILL

1
2
3
4
5

MY NEW HABITS

NOTE:

USE THESE SENTENCE STARTERS TO WRITE AN ARTICLE. COMPLETE ONE, TWO, OR ALL OF THESE LINES BELOW:

- TODAY WAS A GOOD/BAD DAY FOR ME BECAUSE...

- I WAS EXCITED TO...

- I HAD THE OPPORTUNITY TO...

- I DIDN'T EXPECT TO...

DAY 39

Daily Journal

DATE :

TODAY I'M GRATEFUL FOR

MY PRIORITIES

☆ 3 THINGS YOU ARE DOING WELL CURRENTLY

TO DO LIST

- [ ] ______
- [ ] ______
- [ ] ______
- [ ] ______
- [ ] ______
- [ ]

DID YOU DO SOMETHING NICE TO SOMEONE TODAY? WRITE ABOUT IT.

CAN YOU DO BETTER TOMORROW? HOW?

DAILY CHECK-UP

MY MOOD TODAY

1 2 3 4 5 6 7 8 9 10

WHY DO I FEEL THIS WAY?

EDUCATION/SKILL

1
2
3
4
5

MY NEW HABITS

NOTE:

One Day, I Want To

EXPERIENCING AND EXPRESSING EMOTION

WHAT TRUTH WOULD I BE SPEAKING INTO YOUR LIFE TO EMPOWER YOU?

NOTES

AND WHAT IS LIFE ASKING ME TO DO DIFFERENTLY?

DAY 40

Daily Journal

DATE :

TODAY I'M GRATEFUL FOR

MY PRIORITIES

☆ 3 THINGS YOU ARE DOING WELL CURRENTLY

TO DO LIST

- [ ]
- [ ]
- [ ]
- [ ]
- [ ]
- [ ]

DID YOU DO SOMETHING NICE TO SOMEONE TODAY? WRITE ABOUT IT.

CAN YOU DO BETTER TOMORROW? HOW?

DAILY CHECK-UP

MY MOOD TODAY

1 2 3 4 5 6 7 8 9 10

WHY DO I FEEL THIS WAY?

EDUCATION/SKILL

1
2
3
4
5

MY NEW HABITS

NOTE:

Mind Map

EXPLORE THE IDEAS

Notoes

Notoes

Notoes

Made in the USA
Las Vegas, NV
27 December 2021

39667310R00109